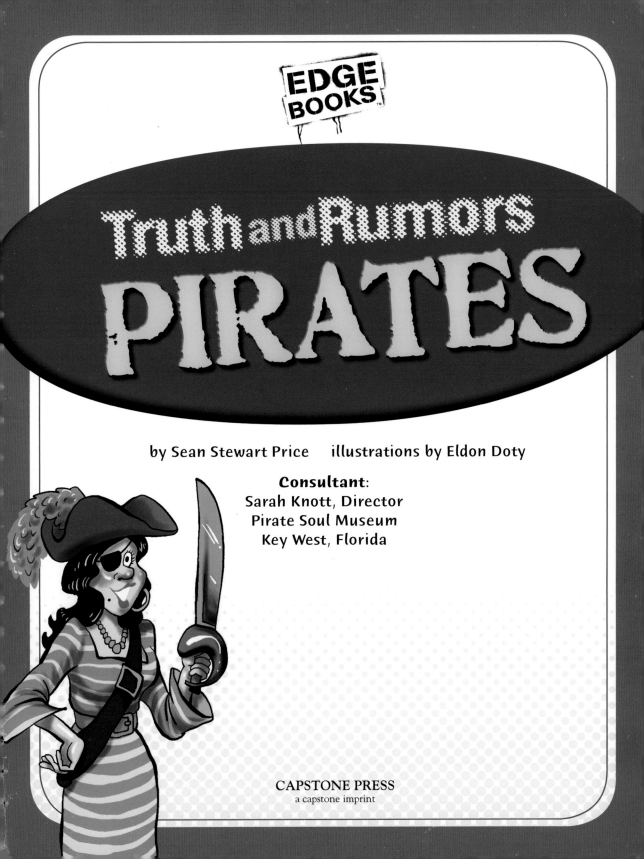

EDGE BOOKS™

Truth and Rumors
PIRATES

by Sean Stewart Price   illustrations by Eldon Doty

Consultant:
Sarah Knott, Director
Pirate Soul Museum
Key West, Florida

CAPSTONE PRESS
a capstone imprint

Edge Books are published by Capstone Press,
151 Good Counsel Drive, P.O. Box 669, Mankato, Minnesota 56002.
www.capstonepub.com

Printed in the United States of America in North Mankato, Minnesota.
032010
005740CGF10

Books published by Capstone Press are manufactured with paper
containing at least 10 percent post-consumer waste.

Library of Congress Cataloging-in-Publication Data
Price, Sean
    Pirates: truth and rumors / by Sean Stewart Price.
    p. cm.—(Edge books. Truth and rumors)
    Summary: "Labels common stories about pirates as fact or fiction and teaches readers how to
tell the difference between truth and rumors"—Provided by publisher.
    Includes bibliographical references and index.
    ISBN 978-1-4296-4746-5 (library binding)
    1. Pirates—Juvenile literature. I. Title. II. Series.
G535.P717 2011
910.4'5—dc22   2009050394

Editorial Credits
Aaron Sautter and Kathryn Clay, editors; Tracy Davies; designer; Marcie Spence, media researcher;
    Nathan Gassman, art director; Laura Manthe, production specialist

Photo Credits
Art Resource, N.Y./Reunion des Musees Nationaux, 26
Capstone Press, 21 (bottom)
Christie's Images/The Bridgeman Art Library International, 8
Delaware Art Museum, Wilmington, USA/The Bridgeman Art Library, 14; The Bridgeman
    Art Library International, 16 (bottom)
ES-Globe Photos, Inc., 22
Getty Images Inc./Apic, 24; Howard Pyle/The Bridgeman Art Library, 12 (top);
    Hulton Archive, 7, 21 (top); Jean Leon Jerome Ferris/The Bridgeman Art Library, 18 (top)
Globe Photos/Alpha, 23
iStockphoto/jgroup, cover (left)
Jason Zalasky/U.S. Navy via Getty Images, 9
Mary Evans Picture Library, 27, 28, 29 (both)
Newscom/Alex Garcia/Chicago Tribune/MCT, 25; Touchstone Pictures, 12 (bottom)
Peter Newark Historical Pictures/The Bridgeman Art Library, 11; The Bridgeman Art
    Library International 16 (top), 18 (bottom)
Shutterstock/c., cover (bottom right); Maciej Mamro, 10; Maugli, cover (background);
    RCPPHOTO, cover (right); Valentin Agapov, cover (background)

Table of Contents

Pirates: What's the Real Story?

Raiding ships, capturing treasure, and looking for adventure. This is how we imagine most pirates lived during the Golden Age of Piracy. But are all the stories about daring pirates real? Here are two tales about swashbuckling pirates. Try to decide which one is true.

1. In March 1579, English pirate Francis Drake captured a Spanish treasure ship. It carried at least 80 pounds (36 kilograms) of gold and 20 tons (18 metric tons) of silver. It was the biggest treasure ever caught by a pirate at the time. Drake's haul was so impressive that he was welcomed home as a hero.

2. In 1720, French pirate "Long Jean" Bartolomeo captured the British city of Port Royal in Jamaica. His crew carted away a large number of slaves. He also captured a shipment of gold that was meant to pay British soldiers. But he didn't enjoy his success for long. He was killed just three days later by a member of his own crew.

Both stories could be true. But which one is? Pirates were some of the most colorful characters to sail the seas. They were also criminals. True tales about pirates can be wild enough. But made-up books and movies make it hard to sort out fact from **fiction**.

This book looks at some of the best-known myths and legends about pirates. It also explores the strange-but-true tales that make pirates so exciting to read about.

fiction—a story about characters or events that are not real

Answers:
1. True;
2. False

Did pirates really say "arrr" and "matey"?

What's the story?

Pirates often talked like rough sailors. They said things like "arrr," "scurvy dog," and "matey."

Arrr!

And arrr to you too!

NOT SO FAST . . .

Some words, such as "matey," probably were used by pirates. They were common terms used by all sailors at the time.

But many pirate words are inventions of actors or writers. For example, it's unlikely any pirate ever actually said "arrr." The term was first heard in early pirate movies, and it has been used ever since.

How to Talk Like a Pirate

Sometimes. Many pirate sayings were created for modern books and movies. But some phrases were used by all sailors. Below are a few terms commonly used by sailors in the 1600s and 1700s.

THE BUCCANEER

swab—a fool or ignorant person

avast—stop

on the account—taking up the pirate life

shanty—a sea song

Were pirates active only in the 1600s and 1700s?

What's the story?

Pirates sailed and plundered only during the late 1600s and early 1700s. They usually raided ships in the Caribbean Sea and off the east coast of the United States.

BUT CONSIDER THIS . . .

Pirates have been around as long as people have been sailing ships. The ancient Egyptians, Greeks, and Romans all had to fight pirates in the Mediterranean Sea. Pirates were often a problem off the coasts of China and India too.

The VERDICT

No. The 1600s and 1700s are often called the Golden Age of Piracy. Pirates had the most success during this period in history. Rich Spanish treasure ships and Caribbean towns were often targets of pirates. But pirates were raiding ships and stealing treasures long before this time.

> **FACT:** In the year 75 BC, Roman leader Julius Caesar was captured by pirates in the Mediterranean Sea. They freed him only after his family paid a large ransom. Caesar promised to later come back and kill the pirates. It was a promise he kept.

Modern Pirates

Pirates still raid ships today. In fact, pirates are a serious problem off the coast of Africa. Lawless pirates often capture huge cargo ships. The pirates demand millions of dollars to release the ships.

Did all pirates fly the same pirate flag?

What's the story?

Pirates always sailed under a black flag with the image of a white skull and crossbones.

WAIT A SECOND . . .

Most of the time, pirates flew flags from different countries so their victims would not suspect that they were pirates. They raised their pirate flags only at the last minute, when their victims had no way to escape. Scared people were less likely to fight back when under attack.

No. Many pirate ships had their own flag design. The flags weren't always black, and many different symbols were used. But the symbols all carried the same basic message—death! Sometimes an hourglass was used to show that the victims' time was running out. Other symbols included swords and skeletons.

> **FACT:** Pirate flags were often called "Jolly Rogers." The name comes from the French term *jolie rouge*, which means "pretty red." Most of the original pirate flags were blood red rather than black.

A. Walter Kennedy; B. Christopher Moody; C. Edward England; D. Henry Every; E. Christopher Condent; F. "Calico Jack" Rackham; G. "Black Bart" Roberts; H. Blackbeard; I. Edward Low

Flags used by famous pirates

11

Did pirates make captives walk the plank?

What's the story?

Pirates made their captives walk off a short board or plank. The victims would fall into the sea and drown in a watery grave.

NOT SO FAST...

Some pirate movies show pirates poking swords at captives until they fall into the ocean. But this image was made up by Hollywood filmmakers. Instead, pirates found simpler and often painful ways to punish or kill their captives.

No. Pirates didn't force their victims to walk the plank. Instead, captives were simply thrown overboard to drown or be eaten by sharks.

A Terrible Punishment

Perhaps the worst punishment on a ship was keelhauling. A man was tied to a rope and thrown overboard. Then he was dragged across the bottom of the ship. Small sea animals called barnacles often attach themselves to the bottoms of ships. Barnacles have razor-sharp shells that can cause painful cuts.

Keelhauling often killed a victim. If the man didn't drown, his body would be severely battered. The victim's wounds often became **infected**, which could lead to death.

Navy captains often used keelhauling to punish sailors. Many pirates were men who had left the navy. They disliked the cruel practice. Keelhauling was not common on most pirate ships.

infected–filled with germs or viruses

Did pirates maroon people?

What's the story?

Pirates marooned shipmates as punishment if they broke the rules. A pirate would be left on a deserted island with only a small amount of food and water.

CONSIDER THIS...

During the Golden Age of Piracy, the world's navies were very strict. Even a small mistake could lead to a man getting beaten, whipped, or worse. But pirate life was very **democratic**. Pirate crews even elected their own captains.

However, even pirates had rules to follow. On most ships, pirates were not allowed to steal from their shipmates. A pirate who broke this rule could expect a terrible punishment. Many movies show pirates being marooned.

You've violated rule number 14—failure to wear an eyepatch and earring!

Pirate Rules

democratic—having a system in which people vote for their leaders

14

Yes. Life on board a pirate ship was often less harsh and strict than on navy ships. However, pirates could be marooned for breaking the rules. Being marooned almost always meant death. Few pirates ever survived this punishment.

The Pirate Code

Pirates didn't all follow an official code. But they did agree to obey certain rules on their ship. Here are the rules used on Bartholomew "Black Bart" Roberts' ship:

1. Crewmen may vote on important matters and share all food, water, and liquor equally. Any man who steals from a crew member can be marooned or have his nose and ears slit.
2. No gambling.
3. Lights out by 8:00 p.m.
4. Each man will keep his weapons ready for action.
5. No women or boys allowed on board. Sneaking one aboard is punishable by death.
6. Deserters may be killed or marooned.
7. No fighting among crewmen on board the ship. Any fight must be done on land.
8. Any man crippled or injured on the ship will be given a share of money.
9. Captain and officers will get a larger share of any prize.
10. Musicians may rest on Sunday.

Did pirates always fight big battles to capture loot?

What's the story?

Pirates sailed large ships loaded with cannons. They fought big battles at sea to get valuable treasure.

BUT CONSIDER THIS . . .

Pirates were thieves. They snuck up on ships they wanted to capture. A few pirates preferred sailing big ships with many guns. But most pirates sailed small, fast ships called sloops. A typical sloop was about 75 feet (23 meters) long. It could carry about 100 men and 10 to 12 cannons of various sizes.

Pirates liked raiding ships at night. They would first come alongside a ship silently. A boarding crew quickly overpowered any guards and disabled the rudder. Then more pirates could come on board.

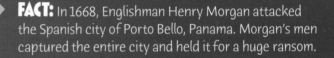

FACT: In 1668, Englishman Henry Morgan attacked the Spanish city of Porto Bello, Panama. Morgan's men captured the entire city and held it for a huge ransom.

The VERDICT

No. Pirates usually didn't like fighting big battles to get the treasure they were after. Most pirates relied on stealth and cunning to capture ships. Most of the time, captives didn't put up a fight. They knew fighting would just get people killed.

17

Was Blackbeard really hard to kill?

What's the story?

Blackbeard was a ferocious pirate. In his last battle, he was shot five times and stabbed 20 times before he finally died.

CONSIDER THIS . . .

Edward Teach, or Blackbeard, was known for his tough and fierce nature. He was a tall man with a long, thick black beard. During battles, Blackbeard liked to carry several pistols strapped across his chest. And he often put long, smoking cords under his hat when he entered a fight. It gave him the appearance of a raging demon.

Yes. Blackbeard was a tough pirate who died as fiercely as he lived. Blackbeard's last battle was on November 22, 1718, off the coast of North Carolina. British lieutenant Robert Maynard tricked Blackbeard and his men into boarding his ship. Maynard's men then quickly surrounded the pirates and killed or captured them. During the fight, Maynard and Blackbeard fought each other with pistols and swords. Blackbeard was finally killed after being shot and stabbed many times.

The Legend of Blackbeard's Body—Exposed!

After Blackbeard was killed, his head was cut off and displayed as a warning to other pirates. According to legend, his headless body swam around the ship several times before finally sinking into the sea.

Is there any truth to this story? No, Blackbeard wasn't that tough. Sometimes bodies twitch and jump around when the head is removed. That may have happened in Blackbeard's case. But his headless body didn't go for a swim.

Did women ever become pirates?

What's the story?

Pirates believed that a woman on board a ship was unlucky. But a few women became pirates anyway. They dressed as men to get hired onto ships. Some women even became pirate leaders.

CONSIDER THIS . . .

There are several stories about female pirates. Some may just be legends. But some are about real people. Two of the most famous female pirates were Anne Bonny and Mary Read. In 1719, both women, dressed as men, joined the crew of "Calico" Jack Rackham. Rackham probably knew he had two women on board. But the rest of the crew likely had no idea.

In 1720, the British navy captured Rackham's small ship. Bonny and Read were the only two crew members to put up a fight. The rest of the crew were too drunk to fight. Rackham and the other male pirates were put on trial and hanged for their crimes. But Bonny and Read were spared because they were both pregnant at the time.

Yes. Women did become pirates, and some of them were quite successful.

Pirate Queens

In the early 1800s, Cheng I commanded a giant force of hundreds of ships and thousands of pirates. Cheng's pirate fleet terrorized the coasts of China and several other nearby countries. When he died, his wife, Madame Cheng, took control of the fleet. She commanded the pirates until 1810.

Lai Choi San was another famous female pirate. In the early 1900s, she was so successful that she became known as "Queen of the Macao Pirates." Lai Choi was a small woman, which worked to her advantage. She made a fortune raiding ships and demanding ransoms.

Lai Choi San

21

Did pirates have eye patches, hooks, and peg legs?

What's the story?

Pirates were men of action. Many were seriously wounded during battles. As a result, many had to wear eye patches and artificial limbs.

THE EVIDENCE

In the 1600s and 1700s, people who lost an eye often wore an eye patch. There was no other way to cover a damaged eye. And if someone lost a leg, a peg leg was often the only substitute.

For Sale:
1 Pirate Costume
Price:
An Arm and a Leg!

Maybe. When pirates did fight in big battles, some likely suffered serious wounds that required eye patches and peg legs. However, it's not clear how common these objects were among pirates. A serious wound to an arm or leg would have required amputation. But such serious wounds usually led to bad infections and often death. Also, pirates had to be physically fit. A person with only one eye might still be useful on a pirate ship. But a man thumping around on a wooden peg leg wouldn't be very helpful.

> **FACT:** One famous pirate, François Le Clerc, was also known as *Jambe de Bois*, or "Peg Leg." He is thought to be the first pirate to use a wooden peg leg during his pirate career. He raided Cuba for treasure in the 1550s.

Pirate Pets

Many people believe that pirates had talking parrots and monkeys as pets. The movie *Pirates of the Caribbean* has reinforced this idea. The truth is that pets would have been messy on board a small ship. Pirates often ran short on food while at sea. Any animals on board likely would have ended up as lunch, rather than kept as pets.

Did pirates bury their treasure?

What's the story?

Pirates didn't want others to steal their captured treasure. They protected it by burying it in hidden locations.

WAIT A SECOND . . .

**Barkeeper
A round of grog
for everybody!**

Pirates were not known for saving money. They often had big celebrations after capturing a rich ship. Tavern keepers in port towns were happy to sell pirates all the liquor they could drink. This sort of high living often cost pirates most of the fortunes they made.

Probably not. Most pirates spent their money too quickly to bother finding a place to hide it. They also tended to keep their treasure nearby so they could keep a close eye on it.

> **FACT:** Pirates did not create treasure maps. The idea of a treasure map with an "X" marking the spot comes from the book *Treasure Island*.

Pirate Treasure Discovery

In 1984, underwater explorer Barry Clifford discovered the pirate ship *Whydah* near Cape Cod, Massachusetts. It is the only confirmed site of a pirate shipwreck ever found.

Since the ship's discovery, scientists have worked to recover and study treasures from the *Whydah*. When it sank, the ship carried the stolen treasures of more than 50 ships. The treasure recovered from the *Whydah* is the only true pirate treasure to ever be found.

25

Were pirates afraid of "Davy Jones' locker"?

What's the story?

Many pirates were afraid to die at sea. They believed they would spend eternity in "Davy Jones' locker."

CONSIDER THIS....

The term "Davy Jones' locker" simply means the bottom of the sea. Being sent there meant that a sailor had drowned at sea. However, the idea of Davy Jones' locker was a little more complicated. Many sailors, including pirates, believed that Davy Jones was an evil demon or a sea god. Some sailors believed they could see Davy Jones during bad storms. He would appear among the sails and ropes of their ships—waiting for his next victim.

Yes. Sailors thought any watery grave meant going to Davy Jones' locker. In fact, the official song of the U.S. Navy includes the line, "Sail on to victory and sink their bones to Davy Jones—hooray!"

FACT: There are several theories about where the name "Davy Jones" came from. Some people believe "Davy Jones" was another name for the devil. Others say it refers to St. David, a saint worshipped by many seamen. "Davy" Jones may have originally been "Duffer" Jones—a clumsy sailor who fell overboard a lot.

The *Flying Dutchman*

Many sailors once thought that the *Flying Dutchman* was a ghost ship that prowled the seas. Any ship that spotted the *Dutchman* was doomed to sink with its crew on board. Both pirates and nonpirates feared seeing the *Dutchman*. Some sailors still believe in the *Flying Dutchman* to this day.

FACT OR FICTION?:
How to Tell the Difference

People love hearing about pirate legends. Pirate life is often seen as adventurous. Pirates are found in several children's stories, such as *Peter Pan*. Even author Mark Twain wrote about wanting to be a pirate when he was young.

There are so many stories about pirates that it's hard to tell which are true and which are made up. Read these stories about pirates, and see if you can tell the difference.

1. In 1700, the British arrested Captain William Kidd for piracy. Some people think Kidd buried his treasure on Gardiner's Island off the coast of New York just before his capture. Today, treasure seekers continue to search for Kidd's hidden treasure.

2. In the early 1700s, British pirate Stede Bonnet captured ships off the coasts of New York and North Carolina. Bonnet once tried to become partners with Blackbeard. But Blackbeard took over Bonnet's ship and left him on a deserted island.

3. Bartholomew "Black Bart" Roberts was one of the most successful pirates of all time. In the early 1720s, he captured more than 400 ships. He was named captain after being on his first ship only six weeks.

Which of these stories is true? They all are! To sort out truth from rumors, do research to get the whole story. Use the Internet to look up experts at museums, history centers, and universities. Call places and ask questions. It's also good to use books and well-known newspapers. Sometimes it's hard to tell if a source is reliable. When in doubt, ask a librarian. Do your research, and you'll have no problem sorting out fact from fiction.

Glossary

amputation (am-pyuh-TAY-shun)—the removal of someone's arm, leg, or other body part, usually because the part is damaged

democratic (de-muh-KRA-tik)—having a system in which people vote for their leaders

fiction (FIK-shuhn)—a story about characters or events that are not real

infected (in-FEKT-uhd)—filled with germs or viruses that cause illness or disease

legend (LEJ-uhnd)—a story handed down from earlier times; legends are often based on fact, but they are not entirely true

marooned (muh-ROOND)—to leave someone alone on a deserted island

plunder (PLUHN-dur)—to steal things by force, often during battle; treasure that is stolen by pirates is also called plunder

raid (RAYD)—to attack suddenly and with surprise

ransom (RAN-suhm)—money that is demanded before someone or something will be set free

rudder (RUHD-ur)—a plate on the back of a boat or ship used for steering

stealth (STELTH)—the ability to move without being detected

Read More

Croce, Pat. *Pirate Soul: A Swashbuckling Voyage Through the Golden Age of Pirates.* Philadelphia: Running Press, 2006.

Platt, Richard. *Pirate.* Eyewitness Books. New York: DK Pub., 2007.

Steer, Dugald. *Pirateology.* Cambridge, Mass.: Candlewick Press, 2006.

Temple, Bob. *The Golden Age of Pirates: An Interactive History Adventure.* You Choose Books. Mankato, Minn.: Capstone Press, 2008.

Internet Sites

FactHound offers a safe, fun way to find Internet sites related to this book. All of the sites on FactHound have been researched by our staff.

Here's all you do:

Visit *www.facthound.com*

FactHound will fetch the best sites for you!

Index